Pablo Escobar

The Life and Crimes of the World's Most Notorious Narco

Table Of Contents

Introduction 3

Chapter 1: The Beginning 4

Chapter 2: Ruthless 11

Chapter 3: Medellín Cartel 19

Chapter 4: Cocaine and the United States 25

Chapter 5: The Family and Colombia 43

Chapter 6: Interesting Facts 53

Conclusion 58

Introduction

I want to thank you and congratulate you for downloading the book Pablo Escobar: **The Life and Crimes of the World's Most Notorious Narco.**

This book contains a complete picture of Pablo Escobar both before and after his rise to infamy.

Here's an inescapable fact: crime is relative. There is not one single definition of good and evil.

If you do not enjoy reading about the justice system and crimes, this book is not for you.

Chapter 1:
The Beginning

So many things about Pablo Escobar are a mystery and his upbringing is no different. There are two stories about how he grew up and where he came from, and no one really knows which is exactly true. Pablo was a man with so much power it is difficult for anyone to really know the truth, so even his early life is controversial. There are two tales about Pablo Escobar's origins, one paints a picture of a life of poverty and a rise to infamy. The other, is a picture of middle class and rebellion that set him down the path of notoriety. Like with many things, it is probably a combination of the two and both stories will be included as they have both been told numerous times.

Everyone has a beginning and Pablo Escobar is no exception. Although it is hard to imagine, he was not always the infamous drug lord people know him as today. As a matter of fact, he had a rather humble start to life as the third child of seven to hard-working parents. His father, Abel de Jesus Dari Escobar was a farmer and his mother, Hermilda Gaviria, a teacher. Pablo was born on December 1st, 1949 in Rionegro, but his family moved soon after his birth to a Envigado, a small suburb of Medellín. Unfortunately, the move did not mean the family was better off financially.

Pablo and his brother Roberto walked more than an hour to school every day. This much walking on one pair of shoes is going cause more than the average wear and tear. Eventually, the soles of the shoes became so full of holes, it was easier to simply take them off. So that is what Pablo did, when his teacher noticed his bare feet in class she immediately sent him home. Pablo was humiliated and told his mother what happened. Saddened by what had happened to her son, she decided that she had no choice to steal the shoes her son desperately needed. However, when she arrived home she realized she had accidentally taken two different sizes. She confessed her crime to the family's priest who urged her to return the shoes, apologize, and ask for the shoes on credit. Hermilda was exhausted after long day of working, shoplifting, and ultimately confessing. When she returned with the shoes she had gotten on credit, Pablo witnessed the state his mother was in from the situation and said to her, "When I am older, I will give you everything."

Growing up this way had a strong influence on Pablo. He knew his mother's father was a wealthier landowner in town, but watched his own mother and father struggle to feed and care for their seven children. His father was often absent, and the burden of the children fell mostly on his mother. She worked all day and then came home only to cook and clean for her family. Of his six siblings, Pablo was closest to his brother Roberto, who was only two years older. Pablo would watch his brother build rudimentary radios instead of playing games with other children his age. Roberto remembers his younger brother as a thinker, generally in his own head, appearing to be deep in thought.

Their mother told the children stories of her father who made most of his money from smuggling whiskey. She told the children of how her father would fool the authorities with his elaborate schemes. Hermilda said her father was very intelligent and always outsmarted everyone, appearing to always be one step ahead of the police. This is something that Pablo took to heart and had a life-long influence on him.

In addition to his unstable and poor home life, Pablo also witnessed his country being divided. When he was younger he saw the effects of the "la violencia" when the country was split between the conservatives and the liberals. This drastic separation led to political assassinations and massacres. The country itself was poor and many people lived in poverty. The environment was looming with the threat of violence, fear, death, and threats. This type of atmosphere would have an impact on any child, and Pablo developed a political conscience early on. In the mid 20th century rapes were performed in the streets in front of fathers, brothers, sisters, and other family members. It was not enough to simply kill a man, instead a ritual needed to be performed, one involving begging, screaming, and usually the brutal slaughter of his family in front of his own eyes. Bodies were badly mutilated and left in public places as constant reminder and used as a way to increase fear. Children were killed on purpose, in slow, torturous ways and heads were left on pikes on the sides of public roads. A common joke among Colombians was that God had made their land so rich and beautiful in every natural way, that it was unfair to the rest of the world. In an attempt to even it out, he had populated it with the most evil race of men.

Pablo grew into these traits, when he was 13 when he became the president of his school's Council for Student Wellness, a group which fought for and demanded transportation and food for the poor. It was during this time that Pablo learned about different types of government, forming his own opinions on the matter and taking anti-oligarchic and anti-imperialist phrases as his own personal mantras. He would repeat these personal phrases for his entire life. It was also during this time that Pablo began to understand the importance of the United States in reference to Colombia. There were rumors that the CIA assassinated leftist presidential candidate, Jorge Eliecer

Gaitan, who fought for social justice. It was this event that led to the separation and violence of "la violencia."

As a young teen Pablo witnessed what happened to those around him and his government. The conclusion he came to was that awful things happened to the poor. Pablo became aware of societal injustices and witnessed firsthand how poverty served as an invitation for misfortunes. Colombia was then ruled by an oligarchy that owned the majority of the country's land and wealth, leaving more than half the country to live in extreme poverty. Pablo hated Colombian society and poverty in general for this reason.

Pablo never lost his drive, ambition, and hatred of a government who would not take care of its people. He swore to those around him that if he did not make one million pesos by the age of thirty, he would take his own life. All of this served as the perfect storm, it created the foundation for who Pablo would grow up to be. His surroundings had an irreversible influence on him and it was his innate drive that would lead him down the path he chose.

Life on the Streets

In school he grew bored and restless, so he turned to the best place he could think of for the education he wanted; the streets. He joined street gangs, hustled and even made some money doing so. After doing this he decided that school wasn't for him and he quit attending classes. The streets taught him the tips and tricks to survive, and how to face and overcome urban cruelty. He spent almost two years on the streets. When his mother found out about this she begged him to return to school, as he only had three years until he graduated. Pablo loved his mother dearly and listened to her advice. However, when he went back to school, he thought his teachers were foolish and their lessons absurd for the type of lives he knew they were going to have to live in a country run how Colombia was. This led to arguments with his teachers and at 16 years of age he was expelled. His mother was furious when this happened, but he just swore to her that even though he was poor now, he would not die that way. He kept telling her that he was going to be big and he meant it.

Even at such a young age, Pablo had an amazing amount of confidence and street smarts. He carried a comb with him and could be seen combing his hair and admiring his reflection in shop windows. During this stage of his life, Pablo had decided that he wanted to be a famous "bandido" and imitated his two heros; American gangsters, Al Capone and the Godfather. He thought that bandits were capable of having a more positive influence on society than the authorities. He also thought that bandits were capable of being more humane, which is something that was important to him. To Pablo, being a bandit was the best way to embody political resistance in an oppressive society. Furthermore, Pablo being Pablo, he would not just be an average bandit, his drive pushed him to be best bandit. It was rumored that he would steal tombstones, sandblast the names off and then resell it.

Part of doing this meant that Pablo routinely broke the law. He did not choose one type of crime either, instead nothing was off limits, he sold fake lottery tickets, ran street scams, sold contraband cigarettes, smuggled goods, stole cars, and even assaulted people. It was also during this time that he began smoking marijuana and would remained stoned throughout the day. Pablo was already a thinker and this just made that trait even more dominant. Those around him noticed that would take long pauses before replying to questions. Most people just assumed it was an impression of the Godfather, when really it was his meditative demeanor and all the marijuana he smoked.

Bigger Crimes

He was 20 when he acquired his first rifle which changed the nature of his crimes. He would use it to casually walk into banks and chat with the tellers as they nervously emptied their safes and drawers for him. Many people thought he was high on something other than marijuana, but the truth was, this is when he simply lost all fear. Just like his grandfather, Pablo relied on his intelligence and seemed unconcerned about the authorities because he managed to always stay one step ahead of them. It was this lack of fear and use of intelligence that made Pablo different than the other thugs walking the streets. He had become a legend on the streets of Medellín, with other criminals and thugs seeking advice from him, many of which joined his gang. It was thought that his unwavering confidence gave his gang members a sense of safety.

Pablo stayed positive and calm, even in the face of danger. While others would become riled up and nervous, Pablo never lost his even tone and confidence. He knew the importance of being deliberate and cheerful. One of his gang members described him as almost God-like and that the day he met him was the most important of his entire life. Even years after his death, Pablo's powerful aura was often discussed.

After Pablo had assembled a rather large gang of his own he dove head first into the most profitable Medellín business of stealing cars which were then stripped and sold for parts. He did so without even getting his hands dirty. He would stay at his home smoking marijuana, giving orders, and collecting revenues. The authorities kept a close eye on Pablo and greatly restrained his illegal business ventures. His members began stealing new cars, but the parts of a new car reported stolen could not be sold, so he did what came naturally to him and bribed the cops. This established his relationship with local authorities, but within a year his relationship with local police chiefs became solid. Any complaints about Pablo selling stolen cars went unattended to, additionally it was those cops who received the complaints that often gave him the new titles he needed to sell the cars.

It is during this time that Pablo's life truly changed. Even with the awful horrors he had witnessed as a child, he was going down a path that made him just as dangerous as the government he despised. No longer was he just a simple street thug and hustler, he was becoming one of most feared men in Medellín.

Chapter 2:
Ruthless

Pablo was in his early 20's when he decided that fear was the cheapest and most effective public relations tool. He used this to advantage to govern the public's mind, usually by killing any obstacles that got in his way. Pablo would murder and kill without remorse, because to him, it was the quickest way to increase his reputation. His is how his motto of "Plata or Plomo" came into being, which stood for "silver or lead." This means that you either accept the bribe or you die by the bullet, hence the use of the two metals.

Pablo knew that building his reputation was a worthwhile investment since it only led to an increase in profits. Curious of how far his reputation reached, he came up with a test. He gave his friends property car titles to cars coming right off the factory floor and told his friends to go pick the cars up using the forged titles. When the factory workers noticed that the titles were fake, Pablo's friends said, "these titles were made by Pablo," and the keys were quickly handed over by scared workers.

Nearly everyone was scared their car was going to be stolen so they began to pay Pablo in order to keep their cars safe. This just increased his profits even more because he was making money on cars he did and did not steal. Pablo's gang began to kidnap wealthy people and demanding ransom. However, even when they received the money they would kill the person anyways. Pablo committed these murders to make a point. His leftist and revolutionary rhetoric from childhood reemerged and he famously said, "In this country where only the poor die murdered, the only thing I have democratized is death."

Pablo Becomes the "Doctor"

It was 1971 and in the Colombian oligarchical government there were many social injustices. Pablo became known as a man who would try to redress these injustices. One of the most notorious figures was a man named Diego Echavarria, a powerful industrialist. He was well-known and widely respected in social circles and wanted to be a philanthropist, he inaugurated schools and hospitals. However, the reality was that he committed many serious abuses; the workers at his textile mills worked long hours in inhumane and dangerous conditions for slave wages, he laid off hundreds of workers without severance pay, he expanded his land by forcefully evicting poor communities, and he killed anyone who would rebel. This forced many people to relocate to the slums in Medellín.

One day it became news that Diego had been kidnapped and his captors were demanding 50,000 pesos. His family quickly gave them the money and thought they would have Diego back alive. It was six weeks later that Diego's body was found not far from where Pablo was born. Diego's body told a story of torture, beatings, and strangulation, Medellín's poor rejoiced. Everyone assumed it was Pablo who had finally brought them justice. This just amplified his reputation and people would shake his hand or even bow down to him, that is how he was given the nickname of "Doctor Escobar." Pablo allowed the rumors and knew he would benefit from it, the death of Diego only increased his profits.

At only 22 years old, Pablo Escobar worked alongside the smugglers he worked for in his teens. Working for smuggler Alvaro Prieto had already made Pablo a millionaire. Pablo's groups brought massive amounts of cigarettes, whiskey, appliances, and clothing into the country illegally through "La

Zona Franca de Colón," in Panama. Pablo's networks also collected smuggled merchandise that came from seaports along the "El Golfo de Aruba." He kept large trucks stationed in each location that would be loaded with hundreds of boxes of merchandise. These trucks had to pass many different inspection points, but due to Pablo's connections, his trucks did so easily.

By the time he turned 25 he already had 40 trucks doing constant business and was both revered and feared. However, like his past continued to suggest, Pablo wanted more. His time of working for other people ended, and he focused on his own network.

The Cockroach

During their many runs to retrieve merchandise, the smugglers in Panama kept asking them why they didn't have cocaine, "Aren't you Colombians producers of cocaine?" they asked. When Pablo learned of this he was skeptical, at the time cocaine trafficking was controlled by the Ochoa brothers, two flamboyant, upper-class boys. Pablo did not trust the boys and especially did not trust their leader, Fabio Restrepo. He also did not think their business was turning enough of a profit.

However, a friend of Pablo's brother Roberto, nicknamed "Cucaracho" or the cockroach, told Pablo that Americans were crazy for cocaine. He told Pablo that they would eagerly spend a fortune for just a few ounces of the white powder. Everyone had heard of the lavish parties being thrown in Las Vegas, Miami, and Los Angeles where people would sniff cocaine all night. Then they also heard of the New York lawyers, doctors, and bankers who would sniff cocaine all day. The hippie movement had swept the United States and it was a time of transition and almost nihilistic tendencies. The younger generation had different priorities than their parents and wanted to experiment and party in new and exciting ways. Now Pablo saw this as a great business opportunity.

Pablo discovered that he could make the same amount of money shipping only a few pounds of cocaine, compared to a truckload of voluminous cigarettes, whiskey, and appliances. And so began Pablo Escobar's journey into the lucrative, but ultimately lethal cocaine business.

The Cockroach also told him of the Huallaga Valley, in the jungles of Northern Peru. The Huallaga peasants had been growing coca plants for decades and this was a major source of coca cultivation. They were masters of growing and harvesting the plant, each night their hands would turn green from collecting the plant. They had an impressive system already in place and could generate a lot of output. He knew those fields were going to be more profitable than a gold mine and he knew that in order to be successful, he needed to get a hold of them.

The Cockroach also introduced Pablo to some Peruvians who were running the cocaine trade at the time. Pablo chose to visit Peru himself in order to ensure that the routes used for the drugs were safe. He also knew that he would be buying and transporting the drugs himself. He was 26 when he obtained his passport to travel internationally. First, he had to pass the Peruvian inspection point on the border in Ecuador. This proved to be an easy obstacle to overcome and he immediately travelled to Lima, the capital of Peru. While there he purchased a small, double transmission Renault 4. He used the small white car to purchase and transport his first kilogram of cocaine. Sticking to what he knew best, when he arrived at the inspection point he bribed the inspections officers.

Pablo, himself described his transition into the drug trade as a modest start. He said he would drive across the country to get one kilo of coca paste, but once he saw how much money he made, he started sending larger and larger amounts of cocaine from Peru to the United States. Soon after Pablo his trucks to bring cocaine from Peru instead of doing it himself in his small car. His trucks could easily pass through the Peru and Ecuador border sites, but extra precautions had to be taken at the inspection sites between Ecuador and Colombia. He had his men stop at the border city of Nariño and load the trucks with sacks of potatoes for camouflage in order to pass through and enter the town of Belen, Colombia.

Pablo rented a house in Belen and filled it with laboratory equipment. It was at this house that the cocaine base was crystallized into pure powder and put into easy to transport bags. These were then smuggled by using common luggage, or "mules" using commercial flights. Pablo had set up a very lucrative deal for himself, Americans would pay 60,000 dollars for one kilogram of cocaine. Soon after Pablo started transporting large amounts of cocaine over the border, his trucks were stopped by the Nariño police and confiscated, his men arrested. Pablo knew the drug trade came with its fair share of risks and didn't really think much of it. However, it happened again just a few weeks later.

Hidden Enemy

That is when Pablo knew someone had to be giving the police information. Pablo and his men began investigating and discovered that his Ecuadorian connections were betraying him. A few days later several Ecuadorian men's bodies were found dead with a banner next to them that said "This is for you to know who you are dealing with."

Shortly after Pablo traveled to Ecuador in order to make new business contacts. It was during this trip that he realized that the Ecuadorian thugs did not know enough to have tipped off the authorities. That is when Pablo realized that he had a new enemy, one that was much more influential.

Pablo's suspicions continued to grow over the course of the next few months and rightfully so. In June of 1976 one of his trucks was seized at the border, and the Medellín police arrested him. He was released because they could not prove anything, but he was convicted for the possession of 29 pounds of cocaine. Pablo spent three months in jail, he got out in September by bribing a judge. He spent his time in jail thinking about who could be working against him. After his release he was confident he knew who it was and set forth with a plan.

Pablo made an effort to contact the Ochoa brothers, but failed on every attempt. Since the brothers were alluding him, he decided to just go to them. Pablo remembered that a year before he had a met a rich young man named Rubin who lived in Miami, but travelled often to Medellín to visit family. Rubin attended college in Florida and while studying had gotten his pilot's license.

The Ochoa brothers, Juan Davis, Jorge, and Fabio were an interesting trio. They spoke English, drank whiskey, organized lavish parties, and thought of themselves as high society in both Miami and Medellín. Rubin lived a similar lifestyle and was considered to be both dashing and handsome, so the Ochoa brothers welcomed him join the gang. Once they learned that Rubin could fly airplanes they hired him to assist in the transportation process. Rubin bought small planes and hired pilots to make the trips to Miami. From Medellín, Fabio sent the other brothers two shipments of cocaine each year.

The Ochoa Brothers

The Ochoa family was considered to be Colombian elite, their father bred one of the best "walking horses" the country had to offer, his horses being worth millions of dollars. However, rumors about the brothers' partying lifestyle, sexual escapades, and connection to smuggling had spread throughout Colombia. When they would visit they were snubbed at the country clubs, and turned away from Colombian private schools. Being treated this way both embarrassed and enraged the family.

In 1976, the Ochoas and Rubin visited Medellín and Pablo contacted Rubin and told him that he could sell his boss 14 kilos of cocaine at a good price. Rubin agreed to the deal and arrangements were made for him to go to Pablo's apartment to make the exchange. Jorge went with Rubin and rumor has it that he was disgusted with the way Pablo looked. Pablo's hair was disheveled and he was wearing sneakers and plain shirt. The apartment was messy with trash on the floor and clothes strewn about. The two rich kids thought he was just a common thug or hoodlum and paid for the cocaine and left.

Taking Medellín

When they took the cocaine back to Fabio's place Pablo followed them. Two months later Rubin and the Ochoa brothers were asked to meet at Pablo's apartment where he told them they were now working for him. When they said no that they already had a boss, Pablo responded by saying that Fabio Restrepo was dead as of an hour before. After the shock wore off they realized that they had drastically underestimated the man they thought to be an average thug. They later admitted that they were terrified of Pablo.

Pablo's notoriety spread quickly after people found out about Fabio's death. Now he was not only intimidating Colombia, but the United States too. He was strict and would only allow things to work his way and only his way. All of this led to what was known as the Medellín drug cartel.

Chapter 3:
Medellín Cartel

Now Pablo Escobar had set himself up to be the head of the Medellín Cartel. Its success was now in Pablo's hands and based on his history of being driven, ruthless, and money-hungry is any indication, the cartel was going to be incredibly fruitful. Between the years of 1976 and 1980 Pablo focused on strengthening his networks and making sure his operations ran smoothly.

Pablo had definitely succeeded in making different and new connections. It was rumored that he had authorities from different countries on his payroll. Many people assumed it was how he was able to build airstrips and use cargo planes to fly cocaine so the United States so easily. Pablo even went as far as staging massive fake drug heists, that showed large shipments getting confiscated by the authorities. Once the cameras stopped filming that cocaine was on plane headed for the United States.

Rubin went back to Florida to finish his education once Pablo was able to take control of the transportation of merchandise. One of the reasons Pablo was able to continue his business for so long was because the United States had yet to get involved. This was a time of the Cold War and the United States had other issues to deal with first. During the 70's Latin America was still haunted by Communism and there will still some dangerous, leftist guerrillas that were trying to overthrow the governments the United States supported.

It was this threat that caused the United States to begin funneling weapons, training and intelligence to destroy these guerillas, like FARC and the ENL. Even so, cocaine was a problem yet, it was still mostly only used by the elite and upper classes, usually discreetly. Of course, there were also the cocaine-fueled parties, but these were also attended and hosted by the rich and were exclusive. However, the United States signed an agreement to extradite narcos, a step that they thought would keep the drug trade under control. In a sentence, they were wrong.

The President of Colombia at the time, Turbay Ayala supported the extradition of narcos, but only for peacekeeping reasons. President Ayala knew of the illegal operations and turned a blind eye. All of the merchandise that was 'confiscated' was still finding its way up rich American's noses. The people of Colombia knew that most of their public works were funded by drug lords. It became just part of their lives, not something they considered to be outrageous at all.

The Hacienda Napoles

Pablo spent 63 million dollars on a large piece of land on the shores of Magdalena River. He spent millions of more dollars building a large, luxurious palace on the property, it could hold more than 100 guests and Pablo hired 700 servants to keep the place running efficiently. The estate had pinball machines, billiard tables, televisions, jukeboxes, bars, tennis courts, a bullfighting ring, and six lakes used for jet skiing. In addition to all of this, Pablo also included a zoo on the property, he had species from all over the world flown to his new home, including gazelles, elephants, camels, ostriches, buffalo, and more.

It was at the Hacienda Napoles that Pablo would throw elaborate parties that attracted the most powerful people in Colombia. Pablo would hire groups of teenage girls as entertainment, making them participate in what he thought were erotic games such as foot races or climbing trees naked. Sometimes these girls were further abused and were forced to shave their own heads and eat insects. The estate even had a gynecological exam chair, used only for sexual purposes.

Not only were these parties meant to entertain the guests, but Pablo also used them as a way to instill fear. During one of his parties a servant was caught stealing silver cutlery, Pablo bound his hands and legs. He then threw him in the pool and forced everyone to watch him drown. He told everyone that was what would happen to anyone who stole from him.

The Common People

One of the things Pablo learned as a child was that the power lies with the common people. Colombian elite seemed to forget this and Pablo used this to his benefit. Pablo gave life back to the areas the government had abandoned and during that time there were many. The country still had a massive population of people living in poverty and the government did very little if anything to help. The Colombian oligarchy only had contempt for the general public, but Pablo wanted to find a way to end their misery. He wanted his childhood dream to become a reality.

Pablo loved the Colombian poor and would often put himself in dangerous situations in their favor. He often said, "Pablo Escobar *is* Colombia, and Colombia *is* Pablo Escobar." For this reason almost everything Pablo did had an anti-oligarchical tone. In 1972, the United Nations hosted a conference warning people about how industries were causing irreparable damage to the environment in the form of pollution and deforestation.

Pablo jumped at the chance to join this movement and founded the program he called "Civismo en Marcha," in which people planted or adopted their own tree. Every Sunday parties were organized in different areas in which the national anthem was sung. Someone working for Pablo, or even Pablo himself, would then give a speech about how important it is to everyone's health to save the environment and preserve the greenery.

Pablo's uncle founded a leftist newspaper called the 'Medellín Civico' which Pablo had used during his rise to power to deliver his messages of justice to the poor. One of the only ways to escape the Colombian slums was through sports, Pablo knew this and built soccer fields, volleyball and basketball courts, in poor areas. He even made sure there were lights so that people could also play at night if they chose.

Pablo strengthened Colombia by means of its most prized sport; soccer. He bought the soccer team 'Atletico Nacional' and paid for them to receive professional training and a more professional infrastructure. If it wasn't for Pablo's involvement the soccer team would not have an international presence. It was only after he paid for their coaching did they qualify to compete in two Soccer World Cups.

The amount of inequality in Colombia was inhumane. A tiny 3 percent of the population owned a staggering 97 percent of country's wealth and land. In Medellín many of the slums next to or even part of dumping sites and the poor collected trash as a means to earn a living. One of these slums in Moravia was visited by Pablo and what he saw he called appalling.

A couple of weeks later a slum in Moravia caught fire and was basically destroyed. The government and the public did send aid or help the area and seemed mostly unconcerned. Pablo could not just sit by and allow this to happen, so he started another program called "Medellín without Slums," it was a civic program that he funded. Pablo and the program built one thousand houses for those who would not have been able to afford it otherwise. That group of houses still stands today and is called "Barrio Pablo Escobar" and it houses 12.700 people.

Pablo did something that even politicians did not do; he kept his promises of helping the poor and gave the poor of Medellín back their dignity. Pablo knew that true power really did come from the masses and the poor people of Medellín loved him even more. To them, he was a shining light at the end of a bleak tunnel. He stood up to a government that allowed children to starve in dumps and gave them nothing. Pablo thought that what was important to politicians did not match up with what was actually important to the average man.

Government and Slow Genocide

The Colombian government, like many other governments gained the monopoly of power and the right to use violence came with that. This same government hid its criminal acts with propaganda messages such as "authority" or "democracy." The truth was they would jail or kill people for simply criticizing it. The poor did not think their own government cared about them at all. They felt that when their government forced them to live a life of poverty and hunger they were committing a crime against their own humanity. The poor people of Colombia believed the government needed to be redressed and that there was no justification of government negligence.

The poor considered the government to be a tyranny that needed to be overthrown. They also knew that in order for them to overthrow the government, death, violence, and cruelty are necessary. This might seem like a radical view, but it is not really. Even theologian Saint Thomas Aquinas thought that certain crimes could be justified, he said if "the subjects being unwilling and forced to accept a tyranny, then in that case, he that kills the tyrant for the liberation of the country must be praised."

With that new perspective, the concepts of crime and violence are relative. The idea of good and evil depends on the outlook of those who judged it. One could argue that Pablo lived his entire life this way. Pablo knew that the way the Colombian government was functioning was only furthering the unequal social structure which would only lead to deaths. A government that fosters such as drastically uneven social structure and fails to provide housing, medical care, and food are committing a slow and silent genocide. Pablo did not want this to happen, which is one of the main reasons he helped as much as he did.

Chapter 4:
Cocaine and the United States

Meanwhile, back in the United States cocaine was no longer only associated with the upper class. It had reached the poor and had created gangs who caused devastation with violent confrontations. These gangs were always fighting to control cocaine distribution. The violence and gang wars worried everyone in America, causing a general feeling of unrest in many homes. To make things even more dire, minorities were consuming cocaine in its cheaper form, crack cocaine and it was causing people to die of overdosing.

Cocaine was being portrayed as a very real and life-threatening threat to American youth. The American public demanded government involvement and President Ronald Reagan made eliminating drug trafficking one if the top priorities. However, no one really grasped the extent of the problem until March 10th 1982 when the police were tipped off about a cargo plane carrying a shipment of cocaine into Florida. Up until then the DEA believed an average of 1322 pounds of cocaine were being successfully shipped into the United States per year. They were in for a rude awakening when they did see the amount that was on the plane; 3,609 pounds of cocaine was on that plane. At the time that was worth more than one billion American dollars. The DEA had been wrong by a very wide margin and cocaine was more of an issue than they initially thought.

That day the United States declared a war against Pablo Escobar.

Pablo Makes a Mistake

It was no secret that at this point Pablo controlled Colombia, he had bought politicians and media outlets and maintained solid connections across the nation. According to most analysts, it was in 1982 that Pablo made the biggest mistake of his life; he left the underground and made himself a public figure. Pablo spent a bunch of money, time, and effort in creating a new public image, one of him as a very successful business man who made a fortune selling and renting bicycles.

Of course, this was not just going to a smooth transition, everyone knew who Pablo was in Colombia and rumors of his drug dealings appeared quickly. Pablo, did not seem concerned with the rumors and the potential it had to destroy his new image. Instead he blamed the ridiculous rumors on the existing government. Most analysts also believed that Pablo would have been able to control Colombian politics from the shadows, but it was unending desire for more that prevented this from happening. Pablo wanted to be famous and have a political career and controlling the government from behind a curtain without the use of his face would not provide him with the level of fame he so yearned for.

Pablo had paid off and funded campaigns from both sides in Colombia. Doing this, he managed to get himself elected as a substitute congressman for Envigado, he would attend meetings when Senator Jairo Ortega was unable to. This was also how he was able to obtain a Visa to visit the United States and diplomatic immunity.

Pablo used his Visa to visit the United States in 1983 with his son Juan Pablo. He had purchased a mansion in Miami that up until then he was not really able to enjoy. He also took his son to Disney World and Washington D.C., there is a famous picture of the two of them posing in front of the White House. That is when Pablo decided that he wanted to be president of Colombia.

This same year, the newly elected Colombian President Belisaro Betancur appointed Rodrigo Lara as Minister of Justice. President Betancur routinely avoided anything having to do with the drug trade, but Lara was brave and loudly denounced the deep levels of corruption and even indicated some Congressmen including Pablo. He went as far as mentioning how they made their fortunes, pointing out the absurdity that Pablo had done so selling and renting bicycles. Lara then confronted Jairo Ortega, the Congressman who agreed and signed to allow Pablo to be his substitute.

Pablo did not foresee or plan for this, he did not know that Lara wanted to ruin his reputation and everything escalated very quickly. Pablo had returned from the United States with the dream and intention of working to become the next President of Colombia, but only months later he heard Lara was frequently confronting Ortega. Lara said, "We have a Congressman who was born in a very poor area, and afterward, through business deals in bicycles, appears with a gigantic fortune, while mounting charitable organizations trying to bribe needy and unprotected people."

Pablo did not know how to respond and chose to react slowly and in a legal way. He also ignored the huge amounts of leverage Lara had counted upon. Lara, with the cooperation of the United States came up with a plan to ruin the hero-worship status Pablo had made for himself. Just like Pablo himself, Lara had powerful friends in high places and stories were written in newspapers uncovering Pablo's shady business practices, shedding the truth on police reports, and publishing the mugshots of his previous arrest in 1976. It only took days for Pablo's dream of a new Colombia to come crashing down.

Pablo sent his men to stop the distribution of those newspapers, but it was too late. Pablo didn't think anyone would not abide by "plata o plomo," that he enforced, he just assumed no one would be brave enough to do so. This ruined Pablo's chance at a political career before it even got started.

1984

All of Pablo's efforts of counteracting Lara's accusations were futile. Pablo accused the Minister of Justice of being paid and helped by the United States, trying to portray him as a puppet to imperialism. However, Colombia's middle and upper classes overlooked Pablo's efforts.

Some pro-United States areas began to associate the Medellín Cartel with the threatening, leftist guerilla of the FARC. This rumor was spread and perpetuated by the United States intelligence to lessen Pablo's popular support. At the same time as Lara was attacking Pablo's image, these rumors resurfaced and Pablo's persona suffered a fatal hit.

Pablo took control of the drug operations again and had people killed if they stood in his way. He did not cut ties with his old connections and used them if he could. This allowed him to revitalize his business. On March 10th 1984, a group of 50 members of the Colombian anti-narcotics brigade and 50 members of the Special Forces from the anti-extortion and kidnapping brigade flew over Caqueta, a remote region of Colombia. From their helicopters they spotted several different camps, exactly where their tracking devices said they would be. A couple of months before, they had snuck two radio transmitters into a shipment of two hundred tons of ether. This is one of the chemicals used in the creation of cocaine. Their creativity paid off and they tipped off the Colombian government.

The narcotics agents thought they had located one lab and were surprised when they realized they had actually found seven large labs hidden in the jungles. The entire compound was ten square kilometers including three aircraft landing strips, a radio communications office, and even a medical center. The people who were working there had their own small houses that had amenities such as showers, televisions, washing machines, and air conditioning. Forty people were arrested and cocaine worth millions of dollars was confiscated. This massive drug bust caused repercussions all the way in the United States; it caused the price of cocaine to skyrocket. This was a shining example of how much control and influence the Medellín Cartel truly had over the American cocaine market.

When the labs were shut down and the cocaine confiscated, drug bosses were furious. Pablo was no exception, he was so irate he admitted that he was more than willing to go to war. Pablo made a connection between the drug bust and the fall of his political career, that connection; Minister of Justice Rodrigo Lara. That is when Pablo had two of his men create a team to assassinate Lara. Young men from the slums in Medellín were recruited.

Lara was not dumb and knew the risks he was taking by outing Pablo and the corruption running rampant through Colombian government. He obtained United States Visas for his children and wife. The threats his whole family received were so violent and intimidating that they lived under different names. United States ambassador Lewis Tambs gave

Lara a bullet-proof vest and demanded he keep it on at all times.

As history has proven, power structures have a tendency to silence the truth since it represents a constant threat. These were perilous times and the price one paid for speaking the truth was generally death. On April 30th 1984, Lara was in his chauffeur-driven Mercedes Benz in Bogota when a hitman on a motorcycle opened fire with a machine gun and killed him. Lara's bullet-proof vest was on the seat next to him. Many think that Lara accepted that the vest was not enough to keep him alive, so he put little faith in its ability to help him avoid what he considered to be an unavoidable death.

Colombia Turns Against Escobar

It was no secret that Pablo was the one that had ordered the murder of Minister of Justice Rodrigo Lara Bonilla, and it was a decision that would cause outrage throughout the nation. Up until this point the Cartels had kept their murders localized within their business practices, such as other gang members and cops. The death of Lara was just a terrifying example of what Pablo was truly capable of. It did not take authorities very long during their investigation to figure out that Pablo was behind the murder, this further outraged the public who demanded the drug cartels be stopped.

The Colombian government reopened Pablo's previous criminal cases. A couple of weeks later Pablo's U.S. Visa was revoked and authorities successfully shut down over a dozen of his coca labs. In a very short amount of time hundreds of chemical drums, seven airstrips, and all of his seven airplanes were all expropriated. In an effort to reduce future complications, Pablo's allies denied any past connections or business dealings with him. The animals in his zoo were confiscated because they were brought to the country illegally. It was when all of this was happening that Pablo made the decision to flee to Panama.

Pablo arrived in Panama to the majority of the Medellín Cartel, including Carlos Lehder, Jose Rodriquez Gacha, and the Ochoa brothers. This had been the plan after the Cartel had been contacted by a Panamanian commander, Manuel Noriega, he told them that through emissaries Panama would be a safe place for their drug trade. Noriega's protection came with a four million dollar price tag, but Pablo agreed to the deal since Noriega was smart and had numerous political connections.

During this time Panama was facing its own set of problems in the form of a political crisis. Omar Torrijos, a graduate of the infamous "School of Las Americas," a U.S. academy for sanguinary dictators, was President of Panama. He claimed to believe in democracy and the poor having rights and his administration was moderate, but still slightly leftist. He was stylish, smoked Havana cigars, drank expensive liquors, and gave thousands of dollars to the poor.

Torrijos and President Jimmy Carter signed a treaty that would gradually give Panama control of the Panama Canal. However, Washington never fully trusted Torrijos because he would say things like, "I don't want to go into history; I want to go into the canal zone." Washington took this to mean that his end goal was to seize the Panama Canal, and for this reason the United States government thought he needed to be removed.

CIA agent General Manuel Noriega received the order to kill Torrijos, and he allegedly placed a bomb in his airplane, killing him in July of 1981. Two years later, Noriega conspired with others in power and became the dictator of Panama, President George Bush supported his rule. However, Noriega followed his greed and did not trust nor favor any side, the only thing that mattered to him was making money. Noriega did business with everyone including Pablo Escobar, the United States government, and the CIA.

Pablo had agreed to Noriega's deal and gave him half of the money before Noriega rose to power. When Pablo told Noriega that he intended to make Panama the center of his operations Noriega did not like the plan. Noriega said the plan was to make Panama a transportation point, but making it the center of operations was never an option. Again, in true Pablo Escobar style, he paid little attention to what Noriega thought or wanted. Pablo's intentions were never to stay in Panama forever, he wanted to lay low and then return to Colombia.

A Return Deal

Pablo searched tirelessly for a way to return home and came up with a way to negotiate his return, he met with former Colombian President Alfonso Lopez and former Minister of Justice Alberto Santofimio. He gave them a message for President Betancur asking for a deal, in response he sent his lawyer to Panama where he was presented with a six-page return proposal written by Pablo. In the proposal, Pablo claimed that he was in control of 80 percent of the drug trade in Colombia and that he was in charge of an operation of more than 100 drug lords. Pablo would agree to shut down his entire trade, and donate all the money, billions of dollars, to the Colombian government.

If he did this Pablo wanted three conditions to be agreed to: first, that the Colombian allow his return, second, the Colombian government does not allow him to be extradited to the United States, and third, Pablo is allowed to keep his personal fortune. Pablo would also agree to substitute the coca crops so the farmers can still earn a living. Pablo was confident that his deal would be accepted, but Minister Lara's murder was not forgotten and still weighed heavily on the public's mind and President Betancur was being criticized for trying to make a deal with a narco. After that, negotiations stopped.

This made Pablo incredibly angry because he felt the people he looked after and helped were turning on him. Pablo made it no secret that he was proud to Colombian and showed, what was his eyes unconditional loyalty. So this behavior from the country and people he loved was simply unforgivable and unjustifiable. From this point on, Pablo would no longer be the same man, he lacked compassion and showed an intense desire for revenge.

By then, Panamanian dictator Manual Noriega already had plans to remove Pablo. Noriega and U.S. President Bush held a meeting with the goal of making Panama a conduit for U.S. money and weapons for the Contras, an army backed by the United States that were fighting against the Sandinistas, a dangerous, leftist guerrilla group in Nicaragua. Noriega thought his connection with Pablo would jeopardize the deal. He decided to shut down Pablo's processing labs, when this happened an irate Pablo called and threatened to kill him. Some people say that he was afraid of Pablo's threats and gave back some of the money given to him, either way, Pablo chose to escape to Nicaragua.

Nicaragua

Similar to many countries in South America, Nicaragua was in a state of turmoil. In 1979, the Sandinistas, a Marxist guerrilla, managed to overthrow the dictator Anastasio Somoza, who was backed by the United States. The Sandinistas created a Junta of National Reconstruction that from 1979 to 1990 prosecuted everyone who was connected to the fallen dictatorship. The Sandinistas were violent and their confrontations with the CIA proxy army, "the Contras," were vicious. The Contras wanted to reinstate U.S. control. Sandinista leader, Daniel Ortega was the supervisor to all political operations during that era, he is the current President of Nicaragua.

Pablo settled in Managua, Nicaragua and continued to direct his drug trade. Pablo's freedom made it obvious that he had made very close ties with Ortega. While he was there pictures of Pablo and his associate Rodriguez Gacha were taken at the airport as they oversaw a shipment of cocaine headed to Miami. These images were not easy to get, with the help of Barry Seal, an American pilot and drug trafficker, who turned into an informant the DEA had a camera planted into the nose of one of the cargo planes. It was this camera that captured the images. This was the first time that they had proof that two of the most powerful and wanted drug bosses were now directly connected to the dope.

These pictures caused chaos in Washington and led U.S. officials to believe that the Sandinistas were funded by drug money. This was a time in American history when foreign policy was focusing on fighting Communism, however once a connection was made between Narco trafficking and Communism, putting a stop to the drug trade became a priority. The DEA wanted the pictures to be kept a secret, but

Washington chose to use them in the anti-drug campaign. This meant that Pablo Escobar was deemed an international threat, he was portrayed as an individual who was undermining U.S. power.

Other than the amount of freedom Pablo enjoyed in Nicaragua, there was no proof that Pablo and Ortega were actually allies. One of Pablo's most dedicated and loyal hitmen, "Popeye," declared that they were indeed close friends and that Ortega chose a house on the Southern highway in Managua an area that the Sandinistas routinely monitored, they were guarding Pablo's safety.

In addition to the house, Ortega allegedly also provided Pablo with the necessary radio equipment and warehouses. He even gave him free reign of a few cargo planes and the local airplane. Popeye said, "Ortega was a man of his word, not like that miserable dog Noriega." Popeye called Ortega a "Narco President," which means that without the drug trade his presidency would not have been a possibility.

Not everything went Pablo's way though, one day the Sandinistas knocked on Pablo's door and asked him for 50 million dollars in order to "help the communist cause." Pablo assumed he was going to be asked to donate some money, just not that much. He was flabbergasted at the request. Needless to say, Pablo was upset, and told them that no one can easily access 50 million dollars. As the days went by, Pablo became more and more anxious, Pablo's life in Nicaragua was depressing compared to the way he was living in Colombia. He thought the country lacked all the amenities he was accustomed to, this caused him to miss Colombia more than ever. One Pablo's main complaints was that the women were not attractive and that he missed the Colombian beauties he was commonly surrounded by.

Fidel Castro

Pablo was determined and never rested on his laurels. He continued to come up with new ways to expand his network and make new connections. He had plans upon plans, always trying to stay one step ahead, so if one of his drug routes was shut down, he had two others lined up as backup.

While in Nicaragua, Pablo thought it would be beneficial to him to approach Fidel Castro. One of the reasons for this is that Cuba would be a good trading point since it had already severed its ties to the United States. Cuba was also close to Miami, still one of the cartel's largest markets. One of Pablo's allies in Miami named Jorge Avendano, or "The Crocodile," was a well-known drug lord in Miami. He also flaunted and enjoyed a lavish lifestyle, fitting in very well with Ochoa brothers. The Ochoa brothers made many connections through their partying habits, many of which were Cuban Americans, such as The Crocodile. This is how, with the use of a third party Pablo was able to reach out to Fidel Castro.

Pablo demanded The Crocodile give Fidel a business proposition, but Fidel was too busy to deal with it himself so he sent his brother Raul. It was through the intervention of Raul that Pablo was able to strike up a deal with Fidel and The Crocodile traveled to Havana to close the agreement.

A new plan and route was set into motion; the merchandise would be transported in various ships from the Buenaventura port in Colombia, the ships would then reach Mexico ports and the shipment, approximately 26,455 pounds each, would be taken to a Mexican airport. From there, Mexican planes would then fly the cargo to Cuba and unload it on the island's coasts. Two of Fidel's closest associates were in charge of supervising the job, colonel Tony La Guardia and Cuban general Arnaldo Ochoa.

From there Cuban soldiers would take the cocaine in smaller boats to Miami, this was part of the agreement with Fidel. Once in Miami, the goods would be taken to one of Pablo's drug lords, a man known as "The Dirt," who would then hide the cocaine in the Ochoa brothers' mansions spread out in Cayo Heuso, Kendall, and Boca Raton. Fidel's cut of the profits means he made around 3,000 dollars for every pound of cocaine that was successfully delivered. Jorge Avendano remained in Cuba, he was in charge of making the payments.

Fidel and Pablo never met, but would converse through letters which were delivered by special emissaries. Even though they never met face to face, Pablo said that due to his work ethic, Fidel was a pleasure to work with. Together, they made a lot of money, an important motivator for both of them.

Returning to Colombia

Even though Pablo could have easily stayed in Nicaragua, but he could not stand to be away from Colombia any longer. He thought that his absence was causing his control in Colombia to be compromised. He knew that some of the drug lords were overstepping and attempting to gain more power. When Pablo received the news that his father had been kidnapped, he knew that his reputation was not what it used to be. In retaliation, he hired some gunmen who were given orders to kill anyone either indirectly or directly involved with the kidnapping. This trail of carnage worked and the kidnappers let Pablo's father go, unharmed.

Late in 1984 Pablo returned to Colombia and swore he never leave his homeland again. One of his most famous quotes is, "I would rather be in a grave in Colombia than in prison in the United States." When he did return to Colombia he found that most of his elite connections were still snubbing him, but he still had some loyal police, soldiers, and sicarios, or boys from the slums in around Medellín , any of which would kill any target if ordered to do so.

Drug lords were now facing extradition if they were caught, because of the mounting pressure from the United States, this was a main focus. Pablo and other drug bosses used everything at their disposal, including bribery and propaganda to influence the extradition issue. However, their attempts were failing and as more and more journalists and judges turned against them, the Cartels methods became increasingly violent. Judges and politicians were intimidated, and as a warning the Cartel assassinated a supreme court judge because he wouldn't abide by their demands. The editor-in-chief of the newspaper El Espectador was murded too. It just so happened, that the day before he was killed, the newspaper criticized Pablo and his associates. The newspaper also made it very clear that they were in support of the extradition laws.

Pablo and other drug lords were nothing if not persistent and the murders continued. In one neighborhood in Medellín the Cartel dumped so many dead bodies that some residents thought it necessary to post signs that prohibited it. It was pandemonium, which is exactly what Pablo wanted. In the face of all this madness, politicians eventually gave in and they changed the legislation. However, the violence did not stop. It seemed that once this line had been crossed a new standard was set. Murder and violence was just now the way to do successful business. Things were quickly spiraling out of control.

Presidential candidate Luis Carlos Galan was assassinated in front of a large crowd in August of 1989. This was a turning point because Galan focused on corrupt politicians and one of main things he was campaigning for was reforms. His death was shocking to everyone in Colombia and from then on, the government just hardened its stance. They decided that there would be no more compromising with anyone, not after the deaths of politicians, especially Galan. For all intents and purposes, the Colombian government took this to mean that Pablo had sent out his own declaration of war. President Virgilio Barco gave a famous speech after this, which was shown on Colombia's national television networks as a live broadcast. He said, "Colombia is at war. We are at war against the drug traffickers and terrorists. We shall not rest until this war has been won." The extradition treaty was reinstated.

The Medellin Cartel's violence became more and more intense and extreme. Between the months of August and December in 1989, more than 88 car bombs were detonated in popular Colombian cities. This explosions, placed at banks, malls, hotels, and offices killed thousands of people. The Cartel also put a bomb on a plane, killing 107 passengers. The term naro-terrorism was coined for these types of attacks. These types of crimes had a huge impact on the public. Colombians began to feel incredibly unsafe, and they were losing faith in their government's ability to take down the drug trade.

"Prison"

Pablo used the violence against the public as a tool to aid in his negotiations, he now had a new position. Colombia was not the only side that was losing men, the drug cartels also lost a bunch of valuable members. It came to the point where both sides just needed a break. Pablo approached the president with an offer, after lengthy negotiations, it was agreed to that Pablo plead guilty to one criminal act and serve out his sentence in a prison that he chooses. In return, the extradition law would be outlawed. So, in June 1991, Pablo surrendered and began to face the music for his crimes, or at least some of them.

When someone talks about doing "hard time," difficulties and being uncomfortable at the very least come to mind, in addition to being surrounded by threats and violence. Well, for a man like Pablo, this just would not happen. He chose the prison called the Cathedral, one of which he built and named himself. It housed some of Colombia's most notorious and vicious criminals. However, the place looked more like a comfortable mansion than a prison. Each cell had its own television, refrigerator, VCR, and stereo. Pablo somehow managed to get his own personnel assigned as the guards. The central part of the house was turned into a massive game room, complete with roulette and billiard tables as well as fitness equipment. Visitors could come and go as they pleased, Pablo welcomed family, friends, athletes, and even high class hookers as his guests.

This outrageous lifestyle of a drug lord in prison irritated the Colombian government, especially after they figured out he had been ordering murders from inside the prison walls. Authorities decided he needed to be moved to another prison, this made Pablo irate and in 1992 right before they were scheduled to move him, he simply checked out of his prison. According to him, the Colombian government did not hold up their end of the deal and broke its promise to him.

With no other options available to them, or so they thought, the Colombian government accepted help from the United States. American agencies and Colombia would combine forces in its hunt for Pablo. This proved to be a difficult hunt because Pablo was continuously moving from one location to another. He was smart and rarely stayed in one place for more than a day. He spent months in the country, but eventually decided to go back to his city of Medellín. The pressure increased daily, and authorities raided hundreds of apartments and houses looking for who they considered to be their arch nemesis.

On December 2nd, 1993, authorities had gotten it right and knocked on the door to his hideout. He ran to the roof and opened fire on them, but when he trying to go from one house to another three bullets hit him, one of which went through his right ear, killing him. Pablo, a man feared by many and enemy of the government, had finally been stopped. The violence from the drug cartels did not. Even today, cartels and FARC are still using violence as a way to do business, putting the public at risk. The violence did not begin or end with Pablo Escobar.

After the death of Pablo, the Medellín Cartel fell apart and the Cali Cartel rose to dominate the cocaine market. The Robin Hood type image Pablo had managed to create had a long-lasting impact in Medellín. Over 25,000 people were present for his funeral as so many people mourned his death. Pablo's wife and daughter were forced to flee Colombia, but were unable to find a country that would grant them asylum. Maria remained loyal to Pablo, but did ask him not to use violence.

Scandals

A television anchorwoman named Virginia Vallejo who had an affair with Pablo from 1983 to 1987 offered attorney Mario German Iguran Arana her testimony in the trial against Senator Alberto Santofimio who was being accused of conspiracy in the murder of presidential candidate Luis Carlos Galan. Iguaran mentioned that Vallejo contacted his office on July 4th, but the judge closed the trial weeks before prospective closing date on July 9th, and Santofimio was sentenced to 24 years in prison.

The DEA took Vallejo to the United States on a controlled flight to ensure her safety. On July 24th, a video of Vallejo accusing Santofimio of instigating and encouraging Pablo to kill Galan was aired on Colombian television. This was considered a key piece of information that allowed Santofimio to gain exoneration and lack of evidence being present in the original trial.

Many of the people Pablo worked for a with were investigated and some of them incarcerated. Even though Pablo was dead, the government still had to deal with the Cali Cartel and the drug trade anyway. So his death did not have the intended result of preventing drugs from leaving the country in general.

Chapter 5:
The Family and Colombia

Pablo's death had an impact on more than just Colombia. He left behind his family and a legacy that they made it difficult for them to be proud. People in Medellín were still grateful for Pablo, he changed their lives for the better, but for the rest of the country who had to witness the war he waged, it was a different story. They remembered the ways Pablo did business, the violence, war, corruption, greed, and danger that was rampant throughout the country because of him. They knew he ordered the death of the politicians and people who were working in their favors. Sons, brothers, and fathers were killed by his men. This is a difficult reputation has caused his family to suffer the burden of Pablo's decisions and the wreckage he left behind.

Pablo's children were only 14 and 9 when they lost their father. In 1989 Pablo was rated the seventh richest man in the world. His fortune was reportedly worth over 25 billion dollars. Pablo's surviving family did not receive any of this fortune because it was seized by Colombian authorities. The family had been welcomed and treated nicely when they had their well-known and feared father, but with him gone their destiny had changed. All they had left were the threats and intimidation from both the public and authorities demanding the repay the damage committed by the infamous drug lord.

It only took months for them not to be able to deal with their precarious situation, so they fled Colombia, desperate to escape. It was not easy for them to find somewhere to stay because the majority of the countries did not accept them. So they moved around, not staying in one place for very long.

Finally, Argentina worked with them and approached Colombia authorities. They brokered a deal and Argentina granted them asylum and even gave them new identities to ensure their safety. Pablo had committed such atrocities that had long-lasting consequences that people did not forget, seeking anyone to blame. The family enjoyed living a safe and anonymous life for a couple of years before someone revealed their true identity putting the family in danger.

What Happened to the Family

Pablo met Maria Victoria Henao Vellejo when she was only 13 years old and Pablo was 24. They began dating immediately, but her family never approved of their relationship. They thought he was beneath them and a common street thug. Two years after they began dating they got married, she was only 15. Pablo was known extravagant affairs and numerous mistresses, throughout all of this Maria never abandoned him.

Despite Pablo's desire for fame and money, he kept his relationship and marriage out of the public eye. No one really knew much about her, but she was known for being infatuated with luxury. She lived the same extravagant lifestyle as Pablo and stood by him during his legal battles. So when the authorities took Pablo's money, she was thrown into a lifestyle she was not accustomed.

When they fled to Argentina she changed her name to Maria Isabel Santos Caballero. Maria and her children lived a quiet middle-class life in Argentina. They had an apartment in Buenos Aires, but old habits die hard, and she still managed to have several housekeepers. It was in 1999 that their identity was exposed. She said in an interview, "I am a prisoner in Argentina for being Colombian. They want to try the ghost of

Pablo Escobar because they want to prove that Argentina in combatting drug trafficking."

In 2000, Maria and her son were arrested and charged with money laundering, it was discovered that she was receiving money from drug lords in Uruguay, of this money was earned illegally. They were both held in jail for 15 months until they were released based on insufficient evidence. This was a longer sentence than Pablo ever received.

The Kids

Pablo's son inherited his first and last name as well as his facial features. This proved to be a dangerous combination when attempting to start over with a new identity. When in exile his new name was Juan Sebastian Marroquín. Even after his true identity was revealed he chose to continue to use his new name.

Juan was always a pacifist and never agreed with the more violent and threatening ways his father conducted business. He still loved his father and there many photos of the two of them together. Juan was born in 1977, so he was old enough in the 80's and 90's to understand the business his father was involved in. Pablo and his son were very close, but Juan made it no secret that he disapproved his father's actions and involvement in the drug trading business. It was actually during a phone call with his son that authorities were able to track the call and they were able to pinpoint his location.

When Pablo turned himself in, he said he was doing in dedication of his son. Juan relocated to Argentina in his late teens and enrolled in school to become an architect. Juan enjoyed living a quiet life without the threat of gunfire and violence, but he was never happy living a lie. His friends and colleagues did not know who he was and he felt immensely guilty for this.

Later in 2009 Juan revealed his identity when he made a documentary called Sins of my Father. He made the film with the help of his mother and two of Pablo's victims of violence and fear. He revealed all of his secrets and he reached out to the Colombian people, Pablo's victims, and even the entire world in order to apologize for his father's horrible actions. Juan is the opposite of his father in that he seeks reconciliation, dialogue, and forgiveness.

Pablo's daughter has remained out of the public eye on purpose and no one knows much about her. There is more information about her as a little girl when Pablo was alive than after. She was born in 1984, and those who were close to the family, they described Manuela as her father's spoiled little princess.

One of the more disturbing examples of how far Pablo would go for his children is when his daughter asked him to get her a unicorn. He bought her a horse and had a horn and wings stapled to the animal. The horse died from a fatal infection from the staples.

When Manuela was little he asked her dad how much a billion dollars was, he said "the value of your eyes, my princess." Pablo also promised his daughter would be the last of his family line and when one of his mistresses became pregnant he forced her to get an abortion. Pablo got Manuela everything she wanted.

In Argentina Manuela changed her name to Juana Manuela Marroquin Santos and at just 10 years old she was thrust into a life without her father who doted on her. She was forced to take public transportation and live in a small apartment. Just five years after, her life was turned upside down once again when their identities were exposed. Today, she chooses to live out of the public eye and she is determined to keep it that way.

The Ruins

Pablo's mansion, Hacienda Napoles" has been converted into a Memorial Museum, an anti-crime museum that is a popular tourist attraction. It is in the town of Puerto Triunfo, 100 miles outside of Medellín. It is considered to a be the epitome of the image change, from the drug capital of the world to a beautiful country to visit while in South America. The place was a lavish playground for Pablo and his elite friends, but now it is a theme park, opened in 2007. The exotic animals are still there and more hotels have been added.

The smaller main house itself has been deemed unworthy of being restored because of the shoddy construction. It has remained untouched and is a common place for children to steal away to for games such as hide and seek. There are numerous framed newspaper articles on the walls as tributes to countless murdered assassinations of policemen, journalists, and politicians. They still hang in ornate glass cases and frames on the walls of the dilapidated mansion.

There are holes in the floors where people had been a quest for finding hidden stashes of cash. For around 6 dollars you can rent a bicycle to wander around the grounds and see Pablo's elaborate collection of classic cars, the airstrips, and through the rest of the park.

There is a tiger pen, which was remade but today is mostly deserted and overrun with stray wires, tall weeds, and bent poles. One person wrote about their visit to the park and described it as grandiose in appearance, but sad because of the treatment of the animals. He was redirected to a small brick enclosure to see the emaciated tigers. When he asked about seeing the elephants, he was told they had died and they were waiting to get a new one.

One of the most popular attractions is a 30-foot-high statue of a pink hippopotamus wearing a tiara. She is a in a flirtatious pose, with fluttering eyelashes. She stands outside an area named Río Salvaje where for 6 dollars you can slide down a winding water slide on a float. The park's real hippopotamus, Vanesa, horses, and monkeys. However, many people say that in contrast to what the website says, the stables are empty and only contain straw and uncleaned straw.

However, the country itself creates the perfect environment for a unique and beautiful experience. There are crocodiles in the swamps and vegetation around tropical climate add an a natural element to the park that is lacking in more artificial safari parks.

There is a water called named the Acuasaurus water park. It looks like a Jurassic Park without the live dinosaurs, with rocks designed to look like it is prehistoric, it gives visitors the idea of what it would be like to swim with the Flintstones. A replica of Fred Flintstone's car is marooned at the end of the pool and brightly colored dinosaurs look as though they were frozen in time when roaming around the edges. A massive hollow octopus is in the middle with its long tentacles acting as the water slides leading to the pool below. The park has not lost all of Pablo's characteristics, anything that can cost money does, lockers are 3 dollars, but there is no food in the café.

Money is spent there, but little money is spent to keep the place running properly.

There is also an African Museum which contributes to the surreal experience. Three statues of native Africans stand 18 feet tall at the entrance, two are holding spears and another has a pot on their head. Pablo also had a large amphitheater built for his own personal entertainment and today it is mostly ignored, the posters lining the walls are the only thing present, featuring images of Charlize Theron to African scenes. The other side of the park is still under construction, and like the rest of Pablo's fallen empire holds potential.

Colombia has made a huge effort to rid itself of Pablo's shadow and influence, and improve its image. Reconstituting Pablo's mansion is just one of the many ways they are doing so. However, there are blatant examples of his work everywhere, from the giant dinosaurs he had built for his amusement to the planes on the property that were used to transport cocaine, they still hang above the park entrance as glaring reminders. It is not the park itself that draws the tourists, it is still Pablo that will remain Hacienda Napoles biggest attraction.

Colombia Today

Colombia has a history of violence and terror, throughout the course of 50 years, guerrillas raped, kidnapped, and killed tens of thousands of people. Today, President Juan Manuel Santos is determined to start a new chapter in the country he calls home. In 2000, a quarter of the land in Colombia was still under FARC control, more than the size of Switzerland. Slowly the Colombian government continued to fight the FARC and took down the first and second in command of the FARC, then 63 of its commanders. This left the FARC with very little land a step in the right direction for Colombia.

President Santos has decided to approach the FARC and the war on terrorism in a different manner, learning from the mistakes of the past. He contacted presidents of other countries affected and has worked on creating a peace treaty with the guerrilla group. However, even during the negotiations he did not accept a ceasefire.

President Santos has said that he studied the necessary conditions for there to be peace within the country. First, the military needed to side with the government. Second, the commanders of the FARC must be convinced that peace would also benefit them and be in their best interest. This is why President Santos made it a priority to make peace with Chavez of Venezuela, with Rafael Correa in Ecuador. President Santos does not agree with either of them politically, but he knows that set of actions is what is best for his country.

The deal does not involve jail time for the FARC, but instead restricted freedom as long as they go in front of a justice committee and admit to their crimes. President Santos is facing much criticism because many people think the punishment should be much more severe. However, Santos thinks that a more severe punishment would prevent them from agreeing to a peace treaty and ending the violence. Colombia has been isolated since Pablo's death and the fighting has yet to end. President Santos thinks that a focus on rebuilding the country and making reparations to the victims and their families is the best way to start.

President Santos has said that Colombia has faced this issue before, he too would like to incarcerate FARC members for their heinous crimes, but in doing so there would not be the peace they seek. This treaty focuses on the line that is drawn between peace and justice. The violence and fighting has been going on for 52 years, it is time it came to an end. The FARC do not want to go to real jail, but most are willing to be punished and judged, this is a start and the basis of the treaty. The country might get the retribution to the degree in which they deem appropriate, but in the end the violence would end and that is what is most important.

President Santos says that he does not want the country to continue down the path it has in the past. He thinks about all the victims, which is the entire population of the country, they have lived through atrocities most people could not even imagine, some of which caused by Pablo himself. Most people though support the agreement, not because they think it is justice, but because they do not want future generations to go through what they did.

Part of the treaty is that the FARC must relinquish their arms to international monitors. President Santos has the support of the United Nations and they are aware of exactly how many arms they are in possession of, and they have no choice but to give them up. If they don't they will lose their benefits.

In addition to this President Santos also included in the treaty a benefit for the FARC. In 2018, they will be given seats in both houses of parliament. They will be given five out of 102 seats in the upper house and five out of 166 seats in the lower. Again, he is criticized for this, but he says that this allows the illegal group to continue their ideological fight, but through legal means.

Even though the group committed heinous crimes, what they have always wanted was to be represented and listened to in the political sphere. President Santos says that he doesn't think they will have too much success because the country has evolved so much throughout the decades and their political discourse is outdated and archaic.

Pablo and other drug lords made sure to keep their operations in remote locations. These locations have been off limits for decades because of both the cartels and the guerrillas. So there was very little the government could do to improve conditions. If peace were to come to the country, these ignored regions could be helped, thus improving the quality of life all around. Pablo was doing this during his heyday, and now the government seems to be looking ahead and taking a page out of his book.

Chapter 6:
Interesting Facts

Much of what we know about Pablo Escobar has been controlled by the media and his publicists. So for a very long time we only knew what he wanted the public to. Over time though, through interviews and extensive research new and interesting facts about Pablo have emerged.

- Rats ate approximately one billion of Pablo's profits each year. Pablo kept a very close eye on his books and profits. His profits averaged about 20 billion annually, he was practical in his book keeping and wrote off 10 percent of his profits due to rats eating it in storage or from water damage in the warehouses. In addition to that he spent 2,500 dollars each month on rubber bands to band his exorbitant amount of money.

- Pablo was a suspect in the 1993 bombing of the World Trade Center, the explosion killed six and injured more than a thousand people. A prosecutor suggested to authorities that the bombing was carried out by an enemy of the U.S. and at the time that included the Medellín Cartel. Pablo committed many atrocities including the assassination of a presidential candidate, bombed a commercial jet, threatened one of President Bush's sons, and even tried to assassinate the entire Colombian Supreme Court, but even Pablo was offended to be accused of this. He sent a handwritten letter to the United States ambassador. Pablo declared his innocence in this and said that if had been the one to do it, he would have publicly said why he did it and what he wanted.

- Pablo was a family man and loved his children unconditionally. When the family was in hiding his daughter became very ill and in order to keep her warm he burned about two million dollars in order to keep her warm.

- The pilots Pablo used to fly cocaine could earn up to 500,000 per day, depending on how much product they were able to successfully smuggle.

- During the war against drugs authorities seized 142 planes, 32 yachts, 20 helicopters, and 141 homes and offices from Pablo.

- During a search of Pablo's home a copy of the famous book "The Power of Positive Thinking" was found in Spanish translation.

- In addition to all of the negative things Pablo did, he still remembered his roots and really did focus on making Colombia better. He created a barrio, donated money to churches and hospitals, built parks and stadiums, and even created a food program meant to feed the less fortunate.

- Pablo also bought an entire island in Norman's Cay, in the Bahamas. This was used as part of a smuggling route. He also built airstrips on the island and a refrigerated warehouse to store the cocaine.

- One of Pablo's most successful labs was a village built on wheels. It employed hundreds of people and included canteens, medical centers, and even schools for the children of workers. It was located on a huge farm in Venezuela and when a flight needed to land the houses and buildings were rolled away exposing the landing strip. Everything was then moved back into place when the strip was no longer needed.

- It was rumored that Pablo supported the storming of the Colombian Supreme Court by the guerrillas known as M-19. Half of the judges on the court were murdered. It was thought that this was committed in retaliation of the extradition law being put into effect. Pablo allegedly paid them to break into the Palace to burn papers and files on the Los Extraditables, well-known cocaine smugglers who were being threatened with being extradited to the United States.

- Pablo's wife Maria was so supportive of Pablo that the Cali Cartel show videos of her and Pablo, telling their women that is how they should behave. It has been said that her attitude saved both her and children's lives, since the new cartel had thought about killing them after Pablo's death.

- Many believe Pablo's widow lives a quiet life in North Carolina, although no one knows for sure. She and her daughter did not participate in the documentary her son made trying to make amends for what his father had done.

- Pablo's sister Luz Maria Escobar also tried, numerous times to apologize to the public for what her brother did. She made many public statements and even left letters on the graves of those he had killed. She also organized a public memorial for the victims on the anniversary of her brother's death.

- Pablo's image and name has been used in many different mediums in pop culture. There numerous movies, books, and television shows about him. However, one of the most surprising is that decades after his death, he is being included in video games as well, Grand Theft Auto: Vice City and Vice City Stories have an international airport called Escobar Airport. In the game Resident Evil: Darkside Chronicles the main character is loosely based on Pablo himself. Video game Scarface: The World is Yours features a conversation between Tony Montana, incidentally one of Pablo's idols, and a banker who references how Noriega stole money from Pablo. In the video game Uncharted: Drake's Fortune the villain admits to selling a forged 16th century ornament to Pablo for his museum.

- The hippos Pablo included in his zoo started off as three females and one male. After his death authorities though it too difficult to remove the animals so they just left them at his estate. Well, nature took its course and by 2007 the animals had become feral and increased to 17. Now there are over 40 and they are being a nuisance to the locals.

- Some people think the bullet that killed Pablo was self-inflicted. His greatest fear was extradition, and he refused to spend any time in an American prison. He reportedly told his son that he would shoot himself in the ear, causing his own death if trapped. That is exactly what happened and his son has gone public claiming that he too believes his father took his own life.

Pablo Escobar will always capture the attention of people. There are numerous movies, books, and even a television show about him and his extravagant lifestyle. Some people remember him fondly and are grateful for what he gave them or the area they live in. Others consider him to be nothing but violent and threatening, perpetuating a life of fear. Either way, Pablo was a real man who did more than what the average man does in a lifetime.

Pablo was so much part of Colombia's history that he will never be forgotten, which is exactly what he wanted. He loved the country he called home and was proud to be Colombian. As much as the country wants to close the chapter on his reign of terror, there are numerous reminders of both the good and bad things he had done. Pablo made sure that his shadow would live on through the things he built. The barrio he built for the poor still stands today and will continue to and no matter how much people want to pretend that he did not create it, they can't deny it. Pablo turned out to be much more than the American men he idolized, he used his natural charm and sunny disposition to rise to infamy. When he said "Pablo Escobar *is* Colombia, Colombia *is* Pablo Escobar," it was as if he could see into the future, because he turned out to be correct.

Conclusion

Thank you again for downloading this book!

I hope you learned a lot about the mysterious man that is Pablo Escobar.

The next step is to read or watch more about him.

Finally, if you enjoyed this book, please take the time to share your thoughts and post a review on Amazon. It'd be greatly appreciated!

Thank you and good luck!

Made in the USA
Monee, IL
22 June 2022